MEASURING THE WEATHER

CHERS... WEATHER WATCHERS... WEATHER WATCHERS... WEATHER WATCHERS

MARI SCHUH

Rourke Educational Media
A Division of Carson Dellosa Education
rourkeeducationalmedia.com

ROURKE'S
SCHOOL to HOME
CONNECTIONS

BEFORE AND DURING READING ACTIVITIES

Before Reading: *Building Background Knowledge and Vocabulary*

Building background knowledge can help children process new information and build upon what they already know. Before reading a book, it is important to tap into what children already know about the topic. This will help them develop their vocabulary and increase their reading comprehension.

Questions and Activities to Build Background Knowledge:

1. Look at the front cover of the book and read the title. What do you think this book will be about?
2. What do you already know about this topic?
3. Take a book walk and skim the pages. Look at the table of contents, photographs, captions, and bold words. Did these text features give you any information or predictions about what you will read in this book?

Vocabulary: *Vocabulary Is Key to Reading Comprehension*

Use the following directions to prompt a conversation about each word.

- Read the vocabulary words.
- What comes to mind when you see each word?
- What do you think each word means?

Vocabulary Words:

- *anemometer*
- *barometer*
- *thermometer*
- *weather vanes*

During Reading: *Reading for Meaning and Understanding*

To achieve deep comprehension of a book, children are encouraged to use close reading strategies. During reading, it is important to have children stop and make connections. These connections result in deeper analysis and understanding of a book.

Close Reading a Text

During reading, have children stop and talk about the following:

- Any confusing parts
- Any unknown words
- Text to text, text to self, text to world connections
- The main idea in each chapter or heading

Encourage children to use context clues to determine the meaning of any unknown words. These strategies will help children learn to analyze the text more thoroughly as they read.

When you are finished reading this book, turn to the last page for an **After Reading Activity**.

TABLE OF CONTENTS

TOOLS HELP US

How's the weather?

Tools can help us find out!

Doppler radar towers help weather scientists watch storms.

MEASURING THE WIND

Weather vanes spin and point.

They show which way the wind blows.

This kind of weather vane is usually seen at airports.

The arrow points north.

So, the wind is blowing from the north.

How fast is the wind blowing?

An **anemometer** shows us.

It measures wind speed.

MEASURING RAIN AND AIR

How much rain fell?

We look at the rain gauge.

One inch (2.5 centimeters) of rain fell.

What temperature is it?

A **thermometer** shows us.

It measures how hot or cold the air is.

-40 -30 -20 -10 0 10 20 30 40 50 60 70 80 90 100 110 120
-40 -30 -20 -10 0 10 20 30 40 50
°C
°F

Look at the **barometer**.

It measures air pressure.

It shows us if the air pressure is rising or falling.

Rain
Change
Fair
28
29
30
31
5
940
950
960
970
980
990
1000
1010
1020
1030
1040
1050
1060

The air pressure is falling.

A storm might be coming!

Scientists study the weather every day.

They are called *meteorologists*.

They use many tools!

WEATHER
WIND
&
STORMS

PHOTO GLOSSARY

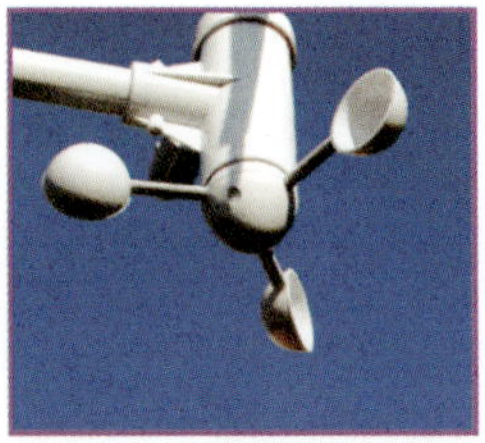

anemometer (an-i-MAH-mi-tur): A tool that measures wind speed. Wind speed can tell us how fast a storm might be traveling.

barometer (buh-RAH-mi-tur): A tool that measures changes in air pressure. Changes in air pressure can tell us how the weather might change.

thermometer (thur-MAH-mi-tur): A tool that is used to measure temperature.

weather vanes (WETH-ur vaynz): Pointers that turn to show the direction of the wind.

ACTIVITY: Make a Rain Gauge

Do you want to know how much rain falls in your backyard? Make your own rain gauge!

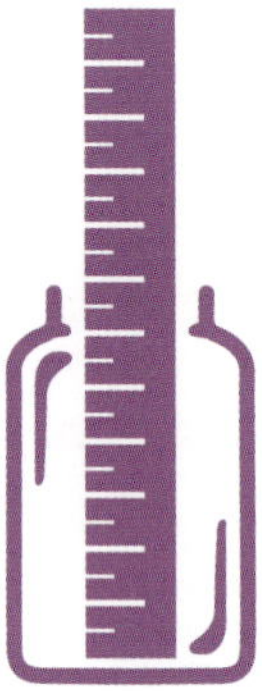

Supplies

large, empty glass jar
plastic ruler
tape
notebook
pen or pencil

Directions

1. Put the ruler inside the jar, so the numbers on the ruler are facing out. Make sure the ruler is standing straight up and down in the jar.
2. Tape the top of the ruler to the jar so it doesn't move.
3. Find a good place in your backyard to put your rain gauge. Check it every day for two weeks. Write in your notebook how much rain fell each day. What day had the most rain?

ABOUT THE AUTHOR

Mari Schuh is the author of more than 300 nonfiction books for beginning readers, including many books about sports, animals, and stormy weather. She lives in Iowa with her husband and one very feisty house rabbit. You can learn more at her website: www.marischuh.com.

INDEX

AFTER READING ACTIVITY

Your eyes can be a tool to help you learn more about the weather around you. Look out a window. What do you see? What are people wearing? Is anything blowing in the wind? Are there clouds in the sky? What does all of this tell you about the weather outside?

Library of Congress PCN Data

Measuring the Weather / Mari Schuh
(Weather Watchers)
ISBN 978-1-73162-845-9 (hard cover)(alk. paper)
ISBN 978-1-73162-834-3 (soft cover)
ISBN 978-1-73162-846-6 (e-Book)
ISBN 978-1-73163-326-2 (ePub)
Library of Congress Control Number: 2019945571

Rourke Educational Media
Printed in the United States of America,
North Mankato, Minnesota

www.rourkeeducationalmedia.com

Edited by: Hailey Scragg
Cover and interior design by: Kathy Walsh
Photo Credits: Cover, Pg 1, 3-23 ©Serjio74, Petrovich9; Pg 11, 22 ©lauriek; Pg 13, 22 ©Patrick Jennings; Pg 17, 22 ©iLexx; Pg 7, 22 ©Kateryna Mashkevych; Pg 5 ©raksybH; Pg 9 ©StockSolutions; Pg 15 ©M00Nkey; Pg 19 ©Anca Milushev; Pg 21 ©mokee81